Coping Skills for Teens

The Ultimate Coping Tools for Teens to Manage Pressure, Feelings, Stress, and Anger (60 Activities)

Bella Clark

A FREE GIFT TO OUR READERS!

31 Secret Productivity Hacks & Anxiety Journal for Teens & Audiobook Full Version

GO TO THE LAST PAGE TO GET YOUR FREE GIFTS!

Table of Contents

Dear Parents,

As an author with a longstanding commitment to understanding and addressing mental health concerns among teenagers, I've witnessed a significant shift in the landscape of adolescent well-being in recent years. It's a shift that we, as parents, cannot afford to overlook.

The challenges our teenagers face today have evolved alongside the digital age. The rise of social media, the relentless influx of information, and the changing dynamics of peer relationships have all contributed to an increase in stress, anxiety, and anger among our youth. In my years of working closely with teenagers and exploring their struggles, it has become evident that they need our guidance and support more than ever before.

This book, "Coping Skills for Teens" is a response to these evolving challenges. It's born from the conviction that equipping our teenagers with the skills and knowledge to navigate the complexities of their emotional well-being is essential. I wrote this book with the firm belief that it can serve as a valuable resource for teenagers, helping them understand, manage, and triumph over the stress, anxiety, and anger they encounter in their lives.

Throughout these pages, you will find insights, strategies, and practical advice tailored to the unique needs of teenagers. It offers a comprehensive guide, addressing topics ranging from mindfulness and effective communication to healthy lifestyle choices and coping with anxiety. It provides tools and techniques to help them build resilience, manage their emotions, and forge meaningful connections with others.
But this book is not just a manual; it's a companion for teenagers as they embark on their journey toward better mental health. It encourages self-discovery, offering exercises and worksheets that promote self-awareness and personal growth. It seeks to empower teenagers with the knowledge that they can take charge of their well-being and find strength within themselves.

In writing this book, my goal is to offer a lifeline to our teenagers, a roadmap to help them navigate the complex emotional terrain of adolescence. It's an invitation for them to engage in self-discovery, cultivate resilience, and foster personal growth. And it's a call to action for us, as parents, to stand alongside our teens, providing the understanding, support, and resources they need to thrive in a world that continually challenges their emotional well-being.

Thank you for placing your trust in me as we work together to steer you and your teenagers towards improved mental health and well-being.

Sincerely,
Bella Clark

Dear Therapists, Counselors, and Fellow Professionals,

This book grew from a profound commitment to address the evolving mental health challenges faced by today's teenagers. The prevalence of anxiety among adolescents is on the rise, underscoring the need for a practical, tailored guide to help them navigate these challenges.

My primary goal was twofold: firstly, to provide teenagers with an independent toolkit for managing their anxiety effectively and proactively; secondly, to offer therapists and counselors a structured framework and evidence-based techniques that could seamlessly integrate into their therapeutic approach.

How can this book enhance your therapy sessions with teenagers? It serves as a supplemental learning resource, reinforcing the concepts and strategies discussed during your sessions. It encourages self-paced progress, enabling teenagers to revisit and practice coping skills on their terms. It fosters enhanced self-awareness through exercises and worksheets, enriching your therapeutic discussions. Lastly, it facilitates real-life application of coping strategies by bridging the gap between therapeutic insights and daily challenges.

For teenagers, this book offers the opportunity for self-guided exploration, self-reflection, and skill-building. It empowers them to practice essential coping skills independently and monitor their progress, fostering autonomy and a sense of achievement.

Additionally, it's essential to highlight the significance of incorporating "Coping Skills for Teens" into school environments. While therapy and counseling are invaluable resources, the unfortunate reality is that many teenagers do not have easy access to these services due to various barriers, including financial constraints, limited availability, or stigma. Schools can play a pivotal role in filling this gap by making this book readily available to students.

In a school setting, this book can serve as a universal resource, accessible to all students regardless of their individual circumstances. It can be incorporated into health education programs, counseling services, or even as part of the curriculum. By doing so, schools not only provide valuable tools for self-help but also help destigmatize discussions around mental health.

Furthermore, "Coping Skills for Teens" can be an instrumental resource for educators and school counselors. It equips them with practical strategies to support students who may be struggling with anxiety and other mental health issues. It offers a structured framework that aligns with their existing efforts to promote emotional well-being and resilience among students.

By integrating "Coping Skills for Teens" into your therapeutic approach, you can empower teenagers to proactively manage their anxiety, ultimately leading them towards greater mental well-being. Thank you for your dedication to teenagers' well-being, and I hope this resource proves invaluable in your work.

Sincerely,
Bella Clark

HOW TO USE

Welcome to your personalized journey through "Coping Skills for Teens" – an exciting handbook specially crafted to help you conquer life's twists and turns with gusto! Get ready to unleash your inner superhero and tackle teenage challenges head-on.

Inside, you'll embark on an epic quest divided into five thrilling sections, each equipped with activities.
The best part? You can choose your adventure! Pick any section that resonates with your current quest for greatness. Each challenge is like a level in your personal game, and you're in control!

And here's the kicker: these exercises aren't just one-time use items. They're your trusty superpowers that you can wield whenever you need them. With each quest, you'll become a more formidable and confident superhero of your own life.

So, gear up, brace yourself for a thrilling journey, and let's embark on this epic adventure together. You've got the power within you – now go out there and conquer the world!

Coping With Pressure:
Beat school stress, family drama, and friendship challenges with confidence.

Coping With Feelings Through Self-Care:
Boost your self-esteem and master self-love like a pro.

Coping Skills for Stress and Anger:
Learn to control stress and anger like never before.

Anxiety Coping Skills Through Self-Reflection and Growth:
Uncover the secrets of anxiety and level up your personal growth.

Coping Skills for Emotional Balance:
Discover the magic of emotional balance.

Coping with Pressure

Introduction

Hey there! You're at a point in life where you're beginning to feel the weight of expectations from all sides. Pressure seems to be lurking around every corner, doesn't it? Whether it's the impending exams, social challenges, family expectations, or the quest for your own identity, you're undoubtedly experiencing various forms of pressure.

Pressure is a natural part of growing up, and it can come from many sources. Let's take a closer look at some of the ways you might be feeling pressured in your life:

1. Academic Expectations:
School can be a major pressure cooker. You're expected to perform well in classes, manage your homework, and maybe even prepare for standardized tests like the SAT or ACT. Your future often feels like it's riding on those grades and test scores.

2. Social Pressures:
The world of teenagers comes with its own set of social expectations. You might feel pressured to fit in, look a certain way, or act a certain way to be accepted by your peers. Social media can also play a big role in this, with its constant comparison and pressure to have the "perfect" online presence.

3. Family Expectations:
Your family might have certain expectations for your behavior, achievements, or future plans. Whether it's pursuing a particular career path or conforming to cultural or religious traditions, family pressure can be intense.

4. Self-Expectations:
Sometimes, you can be your own harshest critic. You set high standards for yourself, aiming for perfection in everything you do. While having goals is great, the pressure you put on yourself to achieve them can be overwhelming.

5. Future Uncertainty:
The future can be a scary place, especially when you're faced with decisions about college, careers, and your life's direction. The fear of making the wrong choices can create enormous pressure.

6. Extracurricular Activities:
If you're involved in sports, arts, or other extracurricular activities, the pressure to excel in these can be intense. Balancing your interests and commitments can feel like walking a tightrope.

To gain a better understanding of yourself, please check the boxes that resonate with you:

☐ **Peer appearance pressure** (e.g., feeling compelled to dress or look a certain way to fit in with friends)

☐ **Social media expectations** (e.g., the pressure to maintain a perfect online image or compare yourself to others on social media)

☐ **FOMO (fear of missing out)** (e.g., feeling the need to attend every social event, even if you don't want to, because you're afraid of missing out)

☐ **Dating and romantic pressure** (e.g., feeling pressured to start dating or engage in romantic relationships because it seems like everyone else is doing it)

☐ **Social cliques** (e.g., feeling the need to belong to a particular group or clique, even if it means pretending to be someone you're not)

☐ **Academic comparisons** (e.g., comparing your grades or achievements to those of your peers and feeling the need to outperform them)

☐ **Conforming to trends** (e.g., feeling compelled to follow the latest fashion or music trends to be accepted by your peers)

☐ **Participating in risky behavior** (e.g., feeling pressured to engage in risky activities like experimenting with drugs or alcohol to fit in)

☐ **Body image pressure** (e.g., feeling the need to attain a specific body shape or size based on societal beauty standards)

☐ **Social expectations from family** (e.g., experiencing pressure from your family to adhere to cultural or religious expectations regarding behavior or career choices)

☐ **Academic stereotypes** (e.g., feeling pressure to conform to stereotypes related to your academic interests)

☐ **Maintaining a certain persona** (e.g., feeling like you have to hide your true feelings or thoughts and put on a different persona in social situations)

☐ **Friendship drama** (e.g., dealing with conflicts and drama within your friend group)

☐ **Social pressure to be "cool"** (e.g., feeling the need to do things you're uncomfortable with to be considered "cool")

☐ **Pressure to be extroverted** (e.g., feeling like you have to be outgoing and sociable, even if you're naturally introverted or shy)

Understanding which of these pressures affect you can be a valuable step toward self-awareness and personal growth.

It's important to know that you're not alone in experiencing these pressures. Every teenager faces their unique combination of challenges. But don't worry, this chapter is here to help you learn effective coping strategies so you can navigate these pressures with confidence and resilience. Let's get started!

Create a Peer Support Circle

Step 1: Identify Potential Members
Reach out to friends, classmates, or acquaintances you trust and who may also be experiencing pressure or stress. Invite them to join your support circle.

Step 2: Set a Meeting Schedule
Decide on a regular meeting schedule that works for all members. It could be weekly, bi-weekly, or monthly, depending on everyone's availability.

Step 3: Find a Comfortable Meeting Space
Choose a quiet and comfortable location for your meetings. This could be a park, a coffee shop, someone's home, or a virtual space if meeting in person isn't possible.

Step 4: Establish Ground Rules
Together with your peers, create ground rules for the group. These rules might include maintaining confidentiality, active listening, and being respectful of each other's feelings and opinions.

Step 5: Share Your Experiences
During meetings, each member takes a turn sharing their experiences, challenges, and feelings related to the pressure they're facing. Encourage open and honest communication.

Step 6: Active Listening
As a member of the support circle, actively listen when others share. Avoid interrupting or offering solutions unless requested. Sometimes, just being heard is enough.

Step 7: Offer Support
After each member shares, provide support, empathy, and validation. Offer words of encouragement and let them know they're not alone in their struggles.

Step 8: Problem-Solve Together

If a member is comfortable with it, you can collectively brainstorm solutions or coping strategies for the challenges they're facing. However, respect their choice if they'd rather not receive advice.

Step 9: Rotate Roles

Consider rotating roles within the group, such as a facilitator or note-taker, to ensure that everyone contributes to the circle's success.

Step 10: Respect Boundaries

Be mindful of each member's boundaries and emotional limits. If someone doesn't want to share something, respect their decision.

Step 11: Offer Resources

Share helpful resources, articles, or books related to coping with pressure or stress when appropriate. This can provide additional support outside of the circle.

Step 12: Maintain Consistency

Stay committed to the support circle by attending meetings regularly. Consistency fosters trust and a sense of community.

Step 13: Adjust as Needed

Over time, evaluate the effectiveness of your peer support circle. If certain aspects aren't working or need improvement, be open to making adjustments.

Step 14: Celebrate Successes

Acknowledge and celebrate each other's successes, no matter how small they may seem. Positivity and encouragement can go a long way.

Creating a peer support circle can be a powerful way for you to cope with pressure and gain a sense of community and understanding. It provides a safe space to share, listen, and learn from each other's experiences.

Set Goals for Balance

Step 1: Reflect on Current Priorities
Take some time to reflect on your current priorities and the areas of your life where you're feeling pressure. This could be school, extracurricular activities, friendships, family, or personal interests.

Step 2: Identify Values and Interests
Think about your values and interests. What activities or goals align with these values? Identifying what truly matters to you will help you set meaningful goals.

Step 3: Set Specific Goals
Write down specific and achievable goals related to the areas where you're feeling pressure. For example, if you're feeling overwhelmed with schoolwork, a goal could be to manage your time more efficiently.

Step 4: Break Goals into Smaller Steps
Divide each goal into smaller, manageable steps. This makes your goals less overwhelming and helps you track your progress.

Step 5: Prioritize Your Goals
Rank your goals in order of importance. Determine which ones need your immediate attention and which can be worked on over a longer period.

Step 6: Create an Action Plan
Develop a detailed action plan for each goal. Define what you need to do, when you will do it, and what resources or support you might need.

Step 7: Set Realistic Timeframes
Assign realistic deadlines to each of your goals and the associated steps. Be flexible but accountable.

Step 8: Monitor Your Progress
Regularly review your goals and track your progress. Make adjustments as needed to stay on track and motivated.

Step 10: Stay Balanced

As you work toward your goals, remember to maintain balance in your life. Allocate time for self-care, relaxation, and social activities. Balance helps prevent burnout.

Step 11: Celebrate Achievements

Celebrate your successes, no matter how small they may seem. Acknowledging your progress can boost your motivation and reduce pressure.

Step 12: Adapt and Adjust

Be flexible and open to adjusting your goals as circumstances change. Life can be unpredictable, and it's okay to modify your goals accordingly.

Step 13: Reflect on Your Journey

Periodically reflect on your journey and how setting and achieving these goals has helped you cope with pressure. It's a valuable learning experience.

Step 14: Practice Self-Compassion

Remember that setbacks and challenges are part of any goal-setting process. Be kind to yourself and practice self-compassion during difficult times.

Use Art Journaling

Life as a teen can be pretty hectic, right? Between school, friends, family, and all those growing-up changes, it's normal to feel the pressure building up. But guess what? You have a secret weapon to help you cope with it—art journaling! This creative outlet isn't about being the next Picasso; it's about expressing yourself, letting your feelings out, and finding your own unique way to deal with the ups and downs. In this step-by-step guide, I'll show you how to start art journaling as a way to ease the pressure and nurture your creativity. So, grab some supplies, find a cozy spot, and let's dive in!

You'll need a few basic art supplies to get started:

- A sketchbook or journal (plain or with blank pages)
- Pencils, pens, markers, or colored pencils
- Watercolor paints or acrylic paints (optional)
- Brushes (if using paint)
- Old magazines or printed images
- Glue or adhesive
- Scissors

1 Choose your space
Find a comfortable and quiet place where you can focus without distractions. It could be your bedroom, a cozy corner, or a favorite outdoor spot.

2 Set the mood
Put on some calming music if it helps you concentrate. Light a candle or incense if you like, but make sure it's safe and doesn't distract you.

3 Reflect on your feelings
Take a moment to think about what's been causing you pressure or stress lately. Is it schoolwork, friendship drama, or something else? Reflecting on your feelings is the first step to expressing them.

13

4 Start creating

Open your journal to a blank page. Without worrying about making it perfect, start drawing, painting, or writing. Let your feelings guide your hand; there's no right or wrong way to do this.

5 Use words and images

Mix words and images to express yourself fully. Write down what's on your mind, jot down lyrics or quotes that resonate with you, and add images or colors that reflect your feelings.

6 Embrace emotions

As you work, you might find some intense emotions surfacing. That's okay. Art journaling can help you process these feelings and release some of the pressure.

7 Experiment and explore

Try different techniques. Use watercolors, make collages with magazine clippings, or experiment with patterns and shapes. The more you explore, the more you'll learn about yourself.

8 Review your pages

After you're done, flip through your journal. See how your entries evolve over time. It's like a visual diary of your emotions and experiences.

9 Be patient

Remember, art journaling is a journey, not a destination. It may not instantly make your pressure disappear, but it can be a powerful tool for understanding and coping with it.

Art journaling is a fantastic way to cope with the pressures of being a teen. It's your canvas to release emotions, express your unique self, and find solace in creativity.

Master Time Management

ABCD Method

Gather your materials
Start by getting a notebook or digital app where you can create and organize your task list. Choose whichever method works best for you.

List your tasks
Begin by listing all the tasks and activities you need to complete. These could be related to school, extracurriculars, chores, personal goals, or anything else on your plate.

Assign each task a priority level using the <u>ABCD method:</u>

<u>A (Most Important):</u> Label tasks that are extremely important and must be done today. These are typically your top priorities, such as urgent assignments or important deadlines.

<u>C (Nice to Do):</u> Label tasks that are not particularly urgent or vital but would be nice to complete if you have time. These are often smaller tasks or activities that can wait.

<u>B (Important):</u> Label tasks that are important but not as urgent. These might include studying for an upcoming test or working on a longer-term project.

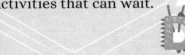

<u>D (Delegate):</u> Identify tasks that you can delegate to someone else, such as a family member or teammate. Delegating tasks can help you focus on your priorities.

Organize by Deadline and Time Required
Within each priority level (A, B, C), organize tasks further based on their deadline and estimated time required. Tasks with earlier deadlines or those that will take more time should be tackled first.

Create a To-Do List
Using your prioritized and organized tasks, create a daily or weekly to-do list. Be realistic about what you can accomplish in a given time frame.

Start with "A" Tasks
Begin your day or work session by tackling your "A" tasks—the most important and urgent ones. Focus on completing these before moving on to "B" tasks.

Stay Focused and Avoid Distractions
While working on tasks, stay focused and minimize distractions. Turn off notifications on your devices, find a quiet workspace, and use techniques like the Pomodoro method (work for a set time, then take short breaks) to stay on track.

Review and Adjust
Periodically review your to-do list throughout the day. If new tasks or unexpected priorities arise, assess their urgency and importance and adjust your list accordingly.

Complete, Delegate, or Reschedule
As you complete tasks, mark them off your list. If you find tasks that you can delegate to others, do so. For any tasks you couldn't complete, consider rescheduling them based on their priority.

Reflect and Plan Ahead
At the end of the day or week, take a moment to reflect on what you accomplished and what could be improved. Adjust your time management strategy for the next day or week as needed.

The ABCD method helps you prioritize tasks, focus on what's most important, and reduce the pressure associated with overwhelming to-do lists. It's a valuable tool for effective time management and stress reduction for teens.

Take a Mindful Break

Whenever you're feeling the heat, remember this exercise. Think of it as your escape button when life gets too intense. Mindful breaks are your opportunity to pause, take a breather, and find your center. They're like mini-vacations for your mind, and they can help you handle the pressure that comes with being a teenager.

In this step-by-step guide, we'll show you how to take mindful breaks effectively. Keep this tool in your back pocket, and whenever the pressure builds up, come back to it. It's your reliable ally in navigating the ups and downs of teen life. So, let's get started, and discover how these mindful breaks can be your superpower for coping with pressure!

When should you come back to this exercise and take a mindful break?

- **before an important exam**
- **after a tough school day**
- **during an argument**
- **when you face peer pressure**
- **when you get overwhelmed by using social media**

Step 1: Find a Quiet Space
Locate a quiet and comfortable space where you won't be disturbed for a few minutes. It could be your bedroom, a cozy corner, or even a peaceful outdoor spot.

Step 2: Decide on the Duration
Determine how long you want your mindful break to be. It can range from just a couple of minutes to as long as you feel comfortable. Starting with 5-10 minutes is a good idea.

Step 3: Sit Comfortably
Sit down in a relaxed but upright position. You can sit on a chair with your feet flat on the floor or cross-legged on the ground. Place your hands on your lap or by your sides.

Step 5: Focus on Your Breath

Begin by taking a few deep breaths. Inhale through your nose, allowing your lungs to fill with air, and exhale slowly through your mouth. Pay attention to the sensation of your breath entering and leaving your body.

Step 6: Scan Your Body

Start from the top of your head and mentally scan down through your body. Notice any areas of tension or discomfort. Try to release any tension you find as you breathe.

Step 7: Ground Yourself

Feel your body connected to the chair or the ground beneath you. Imagine roots growing from your body into the earth, grounding you and making you feel stable.

Step 8: Observe Your Thoughts

As you sit in stillness, thoughts may come and go. Instead of getting caught up in them, simply observe them without judgment. Imagine your thoughts as clouds passing by in the sky.

Step 9: Practice Mindfulness

Bring your attention to the present moment. Notice the sounds around you, the sensation of your breath, and the feeling of the air on your skin. Engage your senses fully in the here and now.

Step 10: Gratitude and Positive Affirmations

Take a moment to think about something you're grateful for or repeat a positive affirmation to yourself. This can help shift your focus to a more positive mindset.

Step 11: End Mindfully

When your mindful break is over, gently open your eyes if they were closed. Take a final deep breath and stretch your body if you need to. Gradually transition back to your daily activities with a sense of calm and presence.

Step 12: Make It a Habit

Try to incorporate mindful breaks into your daily routine, especially when you're feeling pressure or stress. Regular practice can help you stay grounded and manage pressure more effectively.

Mindful breaks are a simple yet powerful way to pause, reset, and reduce stress during your day. They provide an opportunity to connect with the present moment and bring a sense of calm to your busy life.

EXPECTATIONS

Deal Better with Expectations

We know that being a teenager isn't always a walk in the park. One of the biggest challenges you face is dealing with expectations—those unspoken, implied, or explicitly stated hopes and demands that come from all directions. Whether it's from your parents, teachers, friends, or even yourself, expectations can feel like a constant weight on your shoulders.

Think about it. You're expected to excel academically, be socially active, make the right decisions, and plan for your future—all while navigating the rollercoaster ride of adolescence. The pressure to meet these expectations can be incredibly tough.

In this step-by-step guide, we'll help you tackle those expectations head-on. We'll show you how to identify and manage them, so you can breathe a little easier and find a balance that works for you. Let's explore the different types of expectations you might be dealing with and equip you with the tools to cope with the pressure.

Step 1: Self-Reflection
Find a quiet and comfortable space where you can reflect on the expectations that are causing you pressure. This could be expectations from parents, teachers, peers, or even yourself.

Step 2: Identify the Expectations
Take a notebook or use your phone to jot down the specific expectations you're dealing with. Write them down clearly and concisely.

Step 3: Separate Internal and External Expectations
Categorize these expectations into two groups: internal and external. Internal expectations are those you place on yourself, while external expectations come from others.

Step 4: Evaluate Realism
Examine each expectation critically. Are they realistic and achievable, or are they too demanding or even impossible to meet? Be honest with yourself.

19

Step 5: Set Realistic Goals
For those expectations that are realistic and important, turn them into achievable goals. Break them down into smaller, manageable steps to make them less overwhelming.

Step 6: Communicate with Others
If external expectations are causing you stress, consider talking to the people involved. Communication can help clarify misunderstandings and potentially adjust some expectations.

Step 7: Learn to Say No
Recognize that it's okay to say no to unrealistic or excessive demands that are causing you stress. Setting boundaries is crucial for your well-being.

Step 8: Focus on Your Values
Reflect on your core values and what truly matters to you. Align your actions and goals with these values, rather than trying to meet others' expectations that don't resonate with you.

Step 9: Practice Self-Compassion
Be kind to yourself. Understand that it's okay to make mistakes and not meet every expectation. Treat yourself with the same kindness you would offer a friend.

Step 10: Seek Support
If you're struggling to manage expectations and pressure, don't hesitate to seek support from a trusted friend, family member, or counselor. Talking about your feelings can be incredibly helpful.

Step 11: Review and Adjust Regularly
Periodically revisit your expectations and the goals you've set. Adjust them as needed to reflect your evolving priorities and circumstances.

Step 12: Celebrate Achievements
Celebrate your accomplishments, no matter how small. Acknowledge your efforts and progress in managing expectations and pressure.

Step 13: Be Patient
Understand that managing expectations is an ongoing process. It takes time and practice to find a balance that works for you.

Dealing with expectations is a crucial skill for managing pressure as a teen. By recognizing, evaluating, and setting realistic goals, you can reduce stress and make room for a more fulfilling and balanced life.

Stress-Busting Workouts

Exercise is a powerful stress reliever that can help you manage your emotions and boost your overall well-being. These stress-busting workouts are designed to be fun, accessible, and effective for teenagers.

Step 1: Warm-Up (5 minutes)

Begin with a warm-up to prepare your body for exercise. Try these steps:

Jumping Jacks: Start with 30 seconds of jumping jacks to get your heart rate up.

Body Circles: Stand up straight and rotate your shoulders, hips, and ankles in circles for 30 seconds each.

Dynamic Stretches: Perform dynamic stretches such as arm swings and leg swings, for 1-2 minutes.

Dynamic Stretches: Perform dynamic stretches, such as arm swings and leg swings, for 1-2 minutes.

Step 2: Cardiovascular Workout (15-20 minutes)

Engage in a cardio workout to reduce stress and increase endorphin production. A concrete example:

Brisk Walking or Jogging: Go for a 15-20 minute walk or jog in your neighborhood or at a local park. Focus on deep breathing and maintaining a steady pace.

Step 3: Strength Training (10-15 minutes)

Strength training helps release tension and build physical resilience. Here's a simple example:

Bodyweight Exercises: Perform bodyweight exercises like push-ups, squats, or planks for 10-15 minutes. Start with 2 sets of 10 repetitions for each exercise and gradually increase.

Step 4: Mindful Stretching (5-10 minutes)

After your strength training, engage in mindful stretching to relax your muscles and calm your mind:

Yoga or Tai Chi: Follow a 5-10 minute yoga or Tai Chi routine. Focus on deep, slow breaths and gentle stretches.

Step 5: Cool Down (5 minutes)

End your workout with a cool-down to gradually lower your heart rate:

Deep Breathing: Sit or lie down, close your eyes, and take deep, slow breaths for 5 minutes. Focus on each breath in and out.

Step 6: Hydration and Reflection (2 minutes)

After your workout, remember to hydrate and take a moment to reflect on how you feel:

Hydration: Drink a glass of water to stay hydrated.

Reflection: Spend 2 minutes thinking about how your body feels after the workout. Notice any changes in your mood or stress levels.

Regular stress-busting workouts like these can be an essential part of a teenager's coping toolkit. They not only promote physical health but also provide a healthy outlet for stress and anxiety. Incorporate these exercises into your routine and adjust the duration and intensity to match your fitness level and preferences.

Role-Play to Handle Peer Pressure

Role-playing is an effective way for you to practice coping skills in real-life situations. In this scenario, we'll address handling peer pressure, a common challenge for adolescents.

Scenario:
Imagine you're at a friend's house, and a group of peers is encouraging you to try a substance like alcohol or a cigarette, even though you don't want to. Let's go through steps to handle this situation effectively.

 Prepare (5 minutes)

Take a moment to clarify your stance on the issue. Are you comfortable trying the substance, or do you want to say no?

 Initiate the Role-Play (10 minutes)

Ask a trusted friend, family member, or counselor to play the role of your peer. Start the scenario by setting the scene: *"You're at a friend's house, and a group of friends is offering you alcohol/cigarettes."*

 Assertive Communication (5 minutes)

Practice assertive communication by firmly but respectfully declining the offer. Example response: *"Thanks for offering, but I've decided not to try alcohol/cigarettes. I respect your choice, and I hope you respect mine."*

4 Handling Peer Reactions

Anticipate various reactions from your peer, such as persuasion or mockery. Practice staying firm and composed in the face of pressure.

5 Seek Support

In the role-play, reach out to a trusted adult or friend for support. Example response: "I'd rather not, but I appreciate your understanding. Do you mind if we hang out somewhere else?"

6 Reflect

Conclude the role-play and reflect on how it went. Consider what went well and what you could improve in your assertive communication skills.

Role-playing scenarios like this can help you develop the confidence and skills needed to handle peer pressure effectively. Remember that it's okay to say no when you're not comfortable with something, and seeking support from trusted individuals is a sign of strength, not weakness. Practice these skills regularly to build resilience in real-life situations.

Build Resilience With Visualization

This technique can help you manage pressure and improve your performance in stressful situations. Follow these step-by-step instructions to practice visualization effectively:

 Deep Breathing

Take a few deep, slow breaths to calm your mind and body. Inhale deeply through your nose, hold for a moment, and exhale slowly through your mouth.

 Choose a Scenario

Select a specific scenario or situation where you often feel pressure. It could be an upcoming test, a sports competition, or a social event.

 Create a Mental Image

Visualize the scenario in your mind. Imagine the environment, people, and details as vividly as possible. Try to make it feel as real as you can.

 Focus on Your Actions

Now, visualize yourself in this scenario. See yourself acting confidently, making good decisions, and handling pressure with ease. Imagine the positive outcomes.

Engage Your Senses

As you visualize, engage your senses. What do you see, hear, feel, and even smell in this scenario? The more sensory details you include, the more real it will feel.

 Stay Positive

Maintain a positive mindset throughout the visualization. Encourage yourself with affirmations like, "I can handle this" or "I am resilient."

 Repeat as Needed

If you feel pressure or stress building in real life, return to this visualization exercise. Practice it regularly to reinforce your ability to manage pressure effectively.

 Gradual Return

Slowly open your eyes and take a moment to return to the present. Reflect on the positive feelings and confidence you experienced during the visualization.

Visualization is a valuable tool for managing pressure and enhancing your resilience. Regular practice can help you build confidence and perform at your best, even in challenging situations. Use this technique whenever you need to prepare for or cope with pressure in your life.

Make Mindful Decisions

Mindful decision-making is a valuable skill that can help you make better choices when faced with pressure. Follow these step-by-step instructions to practice mindful decision-making effectively:

 Find a Calm Space

Begin by finding a quiet and comfortable space where you won't be disturbed. Sit down in a relaxed posture.

 Grounding Breath

Take a few deep breaths to center yourself. Inhale slowly through your nose, hold for a moment, and exhale gently through your mouth. Repeat this grounding breath a few times.

 Identify the Decision

Clearly define the decision you need to make under pressure. It could be related to school, relationships, or any other aspect of your life.

 Consider Your Options

List all the possible options or choices available to you. Take your time to think through each one without rushing.

 Connect with Your Values

Reflect on your core values and what matters most to you. How do each of the options align with your values?

 Visualize the Outcomes

Imagine the potential outcomes of each option. Picture them as vividly as you can. How do you feel about each outcome?

 **Embrace Mindfulness**

Shift your focus to the present moment. Pay attention to your thoughts, feelings, and physical sensations. Acknowledge any anxiety or stress you may be feeling.

Evaluate with Mindfulness

Review your options from a mindful perspective. Which choice aligns best with your values and feels right in this moment?

Make the Decision

Based on your mindful evaluation, make your decision with confidence. Trust your judgment and the process you've followed.

Embrace the Outcome

Accept the decision you've made and any potential consequences. Embrace it with an open heart and a positive attitude.

Reflect and Learn

After the decision is made, take some time to reflect. What did you learn from this process? How can you apply this mindful decision-making in the future?

Mindful decision-making is a skill that improves with practice. By using this process, you can make choices that align with your values and reduce the impact of pressure on your decision-making. Remember that it's okay to make mistakes; each decision is an opportunity for growth and learning.

Learn to Say No

Learning to say no is a crucial skill for managing pressure and setting healthy boundaries. This exercise will help you practice saying no effectively in various situations.

Self-Reflection

Begin by thinking about situations where you find it challenging to say no. For example, maybe you often struggle when friends ask for your homework answers.

Identify Your Values

Clarify what matters most to you in different areas of your life, like school, friendships, or hobbies. For instance, you might value honesty and personal responsibility.

Understand Your Limits

Recognize your personal limits and boundaries. Think about your physical, emotional, and time-related boundaries. For example, you may need adequate sleep to perform well in school.

Practice Saying No

Imagine situations where you might need to say no and practice saying no assertively but politely. For instance, "I appreciate your request, but I can't share my homework."

Receive Feedback

Ask someone you trust for feedback on your responses. Did they come across as clear and respectful? Did they feel comfortable with your answer?

Reflect on Feelings

Reflect on your own feelings during the exercise. Did saying no feel empowering or uncomfortable? What thoughts or emotions surfaced?

Adjust Your Responses ↻
Based on feedback and your reflections, refine your responses. Practice saying no in a way that feels authentic and comfortable for you.

Set Personal Boundaries ✗
Define specific boundaries for yourself based on your values and limits. For instance, "I won't share my homework because it's not fair to others."

Reflect and Celebrate 🎉
After completing the exercise, take time to reflect on your progress. Celebrate your successes and acknowledge the growth you've achieved in learning to say no.

Learning to say no is an ongoing process, and this exercise equips you with practical skills to navigate situations where you feel pressured to say yes. Setting boundaries and asserting yourself respectfully are important aspects of self-care and personal growth.

Journal to Deal With Pressure

Journaling is a powerful tool for coping with pressure and gaining insight into your thoughts and emotions. Follow these step-by-step instructions to start your journal:

Gather Your Materials
Find a notebook or journal and a pen or pencil that you enjoy using. Make sure it's easily accessible for regular journaling.

Choose a Quiet Space
Find a quiet, comfortable place where you won't be disturbed. This is your private space for reflection.

Set a Regular Schedule
Decide when you'll dedicate time to journaling. It could be daily, weekly, or whenever you feel pressure building.

Prompts for Pressure Journaling
To get started, use these prompts for your journal entries:

Describe a recent situation that made you feel pressure. What happened, and how did you react?

What thoughts were running through your mind during that pressure-filled moment?

How did your body physically react to the pressure (e.g., tense muscles, racing heart)?

Did you manage to cope with the pressure effectively, or do you wish you had reacted differently?

Are there recurring situations or triggers that consistently create pressure for you?

Write about any pressure-relief strategies you've tried, such as deep breathing, talking to a friend, or taking a break. Did they help?

Reflect on the lessons you've learned from past pressure situations. What would you do differently next time?

Write a letter to yourself, offering encouragement and self-compassion when facing pressure.

Begin Journaling
Start writing freely in response to the prompts. Don't worry about grammar or spelling; this is a personal reflection.

Be Honest and Reflective
Be honest about your feelings and experiences. Journaling is a safe space to express yourself.

Set Goals
Consider setting goals for yourself based on your reflections. For example, you might aim to manage pressure more effectively or seek support when needed.

Regularly Review Your Entries
Periodically revisit your journal entries to track your progress and identify patterns in your responses to pressure.

Pressure journaling is a valuable self-help tool that allows you to explore and manage pressure in your life. By regularly reflecting on your experiences and feelings, you can develop a deeper understanding of yourself and build resilience in the face of challenging situations.

Coping with Feelings through Self-Care

34

Digital Detox and Screen-Free Time

A digital detox can be a refreshing break from screens and technology, promoting well-being and reducing stress. Here's how to do it:

1 **Set Clear Goals**
Begin by defining your purpose for the digital detox. For example, you might aim to reduce screen time to improve your sleep quality and focus.

2 **Choose a Detox Period**
Select the duration of your detox. It could be a few hours, a whole day, a weekend, or longer. Make it a realistic timeframe.

3 **Notify Friends and Family**
Inform your close friends and family about your detox plan. This way, they can support you and won't be concerned if you're not available through your devices.

4 **Identify Screen-Free Activities**
Compile a list of activities you can enjoy without screens. For instance, you could read a physical book, go for a nature walk, practice drawing or painting, cook a new recipe, or spend time with pets.

5 **Plan Your Detox Day**
Schedule your detox day and make it official. Clear your calendar of digital commitments like social media or gaming sessions.

6 **Unplug and Store Devices**
On the detox day, turn off or silence your digital devices. Store them in a designated place to reduce the temptation to check them.

7 **Engage in Screen-Free Activities**
Start enjoying the screen-free activities you identified earlier. For instance, immerse yourself in a gripping book, explore the outdoors, create art, or cook a delicious meal.

8 **Reflect and Journal**
During your detox, take moments to reflect on how you feel without screens. Journal your thoughts and emotions, noting any positive changes in your mood or stress levels.

9 **Connect with People**
Use this time to strengthen in-person relationships. Reach out to a friend for a chat, spend quality time with family, or organize a board game night with siblings.

10 **Evaluate and Adjust**
At the end of your detox period, assess how it went. Did you achieve your goals? Did you notice any positive effects? Adjust your future screen time habits based on your experience.

A digital detox can be a valuable self-care practice, helping you find balance and reduce the pressures of constant screen engagement. By periodically unplugging, you can refresh your mind and enjoy a healthier relationship with technology.

Nature Walks and Grounding

Spending time in nature and grounding yourself can be an effective self-care strategy for managing stress and pressure.

Choose Your Nature Setting
Select a natural environment to explore. It could be a nearby park, forest, beach, or even your backyard. Choose a place that resonates with you.

Set Aside Time
Allocate a specific time for your nature walk. It could be in the morning, afternoon, or whenever it fits into your schedule.

Dress Comfortably
Wear comfortable clothing and suitable footwear for walking. Dress appropriately for the weather, whether it's sunny, rainy, or cold.

Leave Devices Behind
Before you start, put away your phone or any digital devices. The goal is to disconnect from screens and immerse yourself in nature.

Mindful Arrival
As you arrive at your chosen spot, take a moment to stand still. Observe your surroundings and breathe deeply. Notice the sights, sounds, and scents of nature.

Begin Your Walk
Start walking at a comfortable pace. Focus on your footsteps and how they connect with the earth. Take deliberate, mindful steps.

Engage Your Senses

Engage your senses fully. Listen to the sounds of birds, rustling leaves, or running water. Feel the breeze on your skin, touch tree bark or leaves, and observe the colors and textures around you.

Observe Nature

Take time to observe the natural world. Pay attention to the intricate details of plants, insects, and wildlife. Notice how everything coexists harmoniously.

Grounding Exercise

Find a quiet spot to sit or stand still. Imagine roots extending from your feet into the ground, anchoring you. Visualize any stress or worries flowing down through these roots into the earth, where they dissipate harmlessly.

Reflect and Appreciate

As you continue your walk or after your grounding exercise, reflect on how you feel. Consider any changes in your mood or stress levels. Express gratitude for the time spent in nature.

Capture the Moment

If you wish, take photos or make a nature journal to remember your experience. Document any observations or insights you gained during your walk.

Return Mindfully

As you conclude your nature walk, transition back to your everyday surroundings mindfully. Carry the sense of calm and connection with you as you re-enter your daily life.

Nature walks and grounding exercises offer a powerful way to unwind and reconnect with the natural world, helping you reduce stress and maintain emotional balance in the face of pressure.

Self-Care Bingo Challenge

SELF CARE is a PRIORITY

The Self-Care Bingo Challenge is a fun way to encourage self-care activities while also creating a sense of accomplishment. Here's how you do it:

Create Your Bingo Card
Using a sheet of paper or a digital document, create a bingo card. Draw a grid with 5x5 squares. In the center square, write "FREE" – this square is a free space.

List Self-Care Activities
In each of the remaining 24 squares, write down different self-care activities. These could include:

- Take a 30-minute walk.
- Practice deep breathing for 5 minutes.
- Write down three things you're grateful for.
- Try a new healthy recipe.
- Listen to your favorite music for 20 minutes.

Personalize Your Card
Customize your bingo card by adding a personal touch. You can decorate it, use colorful markers, or add inspirational quotes.

Set a Timeframe
Decide on a timeframe for completing your bingo card. It could be a week, a month, or any duration that works for you.

Start the Challenge
Begin the challenge by selecting one square from your bingo card to complete. You can choose any square to start with.

Complete the Activity

Execute the self-care activity you selected. For instance, if you chose "Take a 30-minute walk," go for a walk in your neighborhood or a nearby park.

Mark the Square

Once you've completed the activity, mark the corresponding square on your bingo card. You can use a checkmark, a sticker, or color it in.

Aim for Bingo

Continue selecting and completing activities, marking off squares as you go. Your goal is to complete a row, column, or diagonal on your bingo card, just like in traditional bingo.

Reflect on Your Experience

After completing the challenge, take some time to reflect on how it made you feel and the impact it had on your well-being. Did it help you manage stress and pressure better?

Reward Yourself

Celebrate your achievements. Consider rewarding yourself with a treat or activity you enjoy as a way to acknowledge your self-care efforts.

The Self-Care Bingo Challenge is a motivating and engaging way to incorporate self-care into your routine. It encourages a variety of self-care activities and helps you build positive coping skills for managing stress and pressure.

Positive Affirmations

Positive affirmations can be a powerful tool for self-care and boosting confidence. Here's how to use them effectively:

1 Identify Areas of Self-Care
Think about the areas of your life where you'd like to practice self-care. It could be related to stress, self-esteem, body image, or any other aspect you want to improve.

2 Create Positive Affirmations
Craft positive affirmations that relate to the areas you identified. Ensure they are in the present tense and positive. For example:
If you're working on self-esteem, your affirmation might be: "I am confident and capable."
If you want to reduce stress, try: "I am calm and in control of my emotions."

3 Keep It Personal
Tailor your affirmations to your own experiences and feelings. Make them personal and meaningful to you.

4 Repeat and Believe
Begin repeating your positive affirmations. Say them aloud or in your mind. Believe in the words you're saying and let them sink in.

5 Visualize
As you repeat your affirmations, try to visualize the positive outcomes associated with them. Imagine yourself feeling confident, relaxed, or successful.

6 **Consistency is Key**
Make positive affirmations a daily practice. Repeat them in the morning, before bed, or whenever you need a self-care boost.

7 **Journal Your Progress**
Keep a journal to track your feelings, thoughts, and experiences as you incorporate positive affirmations into your self-care routine. Document any changes you notice.

8 **Be Patient and Kind to Yourself**
Understand that change takes time. Be patient with yourself and practice self-compassion. Over time, positive affirmations can help improve your self-care and overall well-being.

Positive affirmations are a valuable self-care tool that can boost your confidence, reduce stress, and improve your mindset. By integrating them into your daily routine, you can enhance your coping skills and build a more positive relationship with yourself.

Guided Relaxation Sessions

Guided relaxation sessions can help you unwind, reduce stress, and promote self-care. Here's how to create and experience a guided relaxation session:

Set the Mood
Create a soothing atmosphere. You can dim the lights, light a candle or incense (if safe and allowed), and play calming music in the background. Choose music without lyrics or use nature sounds if you prefer.

Get into a Comfortable Position
Sit or lie down in a comfortable position. You can use a cushion or blanket for extra comfort. Ensure your body is well-supported.

Start Deep Breathing
Begin with deep, slow breaths. Inhale deeply through your nose, hold for a few seconds, and exhale slowly through your mouth. Repeat this a few times to calm your body and mind.

Set an Intention
Decide on the purpose of your relaxation session. Is it to de-stress, improve focus, or simply relax? Setting an intention helps you stay focused.

Guided Visualization
Close your eyes and imagine a peaceful place. For example, you could visualize a tranquil beach, a serene forest, or a cozy cabin in the mountains. Picture the details and immerse yourself in this mental retreat.

Progressive Muscle Relaxation

Start at your toes and work your way up through your body, tensing and then relaxing each muscle group. This helps release physical tension.

Mindfulness Body Scan

Focus your attention on different parts of your body, starting from your toes and moving up to your head. Notice any areas of tension and consciously release them.

Relaxation Affirmations

Incorporate positive affirmations related to relaxation. For example, "I am calm and at peace" or "I let go of stress and tension."

Deepen Your Breath

Return your focus to your breath. Take slow, deep breaths, and with each exhale, imagine releasing any remaining tension or stress.

End with Gratitude

Conclude your session by expressing gratitude for this time of self-care and relaxation. Open your eyes and slowly transition back to your daily activities.

Guided relaxation sessions are a valuable self-care practice that can help teens manage stress and enhance their overall well-being. Regularly incorporating these sessions into your routine can contribute to improved coping skills and mental clarity.

Gratitude Journaling

Choose your journal or notebook: Select a journal or notebook that resonates with you. Whether it's a beautifully designed physical journal or a digital one on your device, choose a format that inspires you to write regularly.

Find a quiet, comfortable space: Seek out a cozy, distraction-free environment. It could be your favorite reading corner, a peaceful park bench, or a quiet room in your home. The key is to create a space where you can fully focus on your journaling.

Set a specific time for journaling: Dedicate a particular time in your day for gratitude journaling. For example, you can make it a morning ritual to start your day on a positive note, or use it as a calming evening practice to reflect on your day.

Reflect on your day and the positive experiences: Begin your journaling session by thinking about the events and moments from your day. Focus on the positive aspects, even if they seem small. For instance, you might recall a sunny morning, a kind gesture from a friend, or a delicious meal.

Write down the date for your entry: Start each journal entry by noting the date. This simple step helps you track your progress and allows you to look back on your entries to see how your gratitude practice has evolved over time.

List three things you're grateful for from the day: Jot down three things that you feel grateful for from your day. These can range from simple pleasures to significant moments. For example, you might write, "I'm grateful for the cheerful sunshine today," "I appreciate the encouragement from my teacher," and "I'm thankful for the laughter shared with my family during dinner."

Reflect on why you're grateful for each item: For each of the three things you've listed, take a moment to reflect on why you feel grateful for them. This adds depth to your journal entry and helps you connect with the positive feelings associated with these experiences. For instance, you could write, "The sunshine brightened my mood and gave me energy," "My teacher's encouragement boosted my confidence," and "Laughter with my family created a warm and joyful atmosphere."

Express your emotions about the gratitude you're feeling: Don't hesitate to express your emotions in your journal. If a particular moment made you happy, relieved, or content, write about it. For example, you could write, "The sunshine made me feel so happy and alive," or "I felt deeply touched by my teacher's kind words."

Set an intention for the next day: Conclude your journal entry by setting a positive intention for the following day. This could be related to your gratitude practice or any other positive goal you want to work on. For instance, you might write, "Tomorrow, I'll actively look for opportunities to be kind to others," or "I'll begin my day with a positive attitude and focus on the beauty around me."

Make gratitude journaling a regular part of your self-care routine: The key to reaping the full benefits of gratitude journaling is consistency. Make it a habit to write in your journal regularly, whether it's daily, weekly, or on your chosen schedule. Over time, you'll notice positive changes in your mindset and your ability to cope with stress.

Building a Supportive Social Network

You're navigating through a world filled with adventures, opportunities, and the occasional storm. One thing you should never sail without is a strong support network. Why? Because having people who genuinely care about you can make all the difference in your journey through adolescence.

Self-Reflection
Take some time to reflect on your interests, values, and the kind of people you enjoy being around. Understanding your own needs will guide you in forming meaningful connections.

Example: Think about what hobbies or activities make you happy and consider seeking out groups or clubs that align with your interests.

Identify Existing Relationships
List the friends, family members, teachers, and acquaintances you already have in your life. Acknowledge the positive connections you have and the role they play in your support network.

Example: You might jot down your best friend's name, your cousin, or a teacher who always listens when you need to talk.

Expand Your Social Circles
Branch out by joining clubs, sports teams, or community organizations related to your interests. Attend social events and gatherings to meet new people who share your passions.

Example: If you're into music, consider joining a school band or a local music group to connect with fellow musicians.

Nurture Existing Relationships

Invest time and effort in your current friendships and connections. Listen actively, offer support, and be there for others. This reciprocity strengthens bonds.

Example: When your friend is going through a tough time, take a moment to listen and provide a shoulder to lean on.

Initiate Conversations

Don't be afraid to initiate conversations with peers or acquaintances. Ask about their interests and experiences to find common ground.

Example: Strike up a conversation with a classmate about a recent school project or a shared hobby.

Seek Out Supportive Adults

Identify trustworthy adults, such as parents, teachers, or counselors, who can offer guidance and a listening ear when needed.

Example: Approach a favorite teacher to discuss academic challenges or seek advice on personal matters.

Communicate Openly

Practice open and honest communication with your support network. Share your thoughts, feelings, and concerns. Being vulnerable can lead to deeper connections.

Example: If you're feeling overwhelmed with schoolwork, talk to your parents about it so they can offer assistance or guidance.

Be a Supportive Friend

Support works both ways. Offer your help and empathy to your friends when they're facing challenges. It strengthens your relationships.

Example: If a friend is stressed about an upcoming test, offer to study together or provide encouragement.

Attend Social Events

Participate in social events and gatherings, like parties, community service, or team activities. These occasions are great for building connections.

Example: Attend a school dance or volunteer event, where you can meet people from different circles.

Maintain Balance

While building a supportive social network is crucial, ensure you balance your social life with self-care. Take time for yourself when needed.

Example: If you've had a busy week, set aside a quiet evening to relax with a book or enjoy your favorite hobby alone.

Building and maintaining a supportive social network takes time and effort, but it's an essential part of self-care for teens. These connections can provide emotional support, boost your confidence, and make the challenges of adolescence more manageable.

Coping Skills for Stress and Anger

15 Efficient Techniques to Release Anger Immediately

Counting Backwards

1. **Choose a Quiet Space:** Find a quiet spot to sit or lie down.
2. **Start with a Number:** Begin with a high number, like 100.
3. **Count Backwards:** Subtract an increment (e.g., 5) and focus on each number as you count down.
4. **Breathe and Reflect:** Maintain steady breathing, count until you feel calmer, then reflect on your emotional state.

Write an Angry Letter (But Don't Send it)

1. **Express Your Feelings:** Start by addressing the person or situation that has angered you. Write down your feelings and thoughts honestly.
2. **Be Specific and Clear:** Detail the reasons for your anger, using specific examples if possible. Describe how the situation made you feel.
3. **Vent and Release Emotions:** Allow yourself to vent and release your emotions on paper. This can be a cathartic experience and help you process your anger.
4. **Don't Send It:** After writing, set the letter aside. Avoid sending it, as it's meant for your personal release, not for confrontation. Instead, consider other healthy ways to address the issue if necessary.

Squeeze Stress Ball

1. **Hold the Stress Ball:** Take the stress ball in your hand and grip it firmly.
2. **Squeeze and Release:** Squeeze the stress ball as hard as you can for a few seconds, then release. Repeat this action as needed to relieve tension and stress.

Progressive Counting

1. **Choose a Starting Number:** Begin with any number you like. For example, you might start with the number 1.
2. **Count Sequentially:** Count each number in sequence, one after the other, without skipping any. Pay close attention to each number as you say it or think it in your mind.
3. **Continue Until Calmer:** Keep counting sequentially until you feel calmer or more in control of your emotions. There's no specific endpoint; you can stop when you feel ready.

Take a Mindful Walk

1. **Begin Walking Slowly:** Start walking at a slow and comfortable pace, paying attention to each step you take.
2. **Focus on Sensations:** As you walk, pay close attention to the physical sensations of walking—feel your feet lifting, moving, and touching the ground.
3. **Engage Your Senses:** Use your senses to stay present. Notice the sounds, smells, and sights around you. Let go of distracting thoughts and stay fully engaged in the walk.

Guided Imagery

1. **Listen to Guidance:** Listen to a guided imagery audio or video that leads you through a peaceful or calming scenario. Pay close attention to the instructions. (You can find guided imagery audios and videos on platforms like YouTube, meditation apps, and wellness websites.)
2. **Visualize and Relax:** Close your eyes and follow the guidance, using your imagination to vividly picture the scenario. Focus on relaxation and the positive feelings it generates.

Coloring or Drawing

1. **Prepare Your Materials:** Gather coloring materials or drawing supplies such as paper, colored pencils, markers, or crayons.
2. **Choose Reductive Colors:** Opt for colors that may help you manage anger, like calming blues or soothing greens. Avoid using aggressive colors like red or black.
3. **Focus and Express:** While coloring or drawing, concentrate on your feelings of anger and visualize them being transferred onto the paper. Use this creative outlet to release and transform your anger into a more manageable form.

Deep Breathing

1. Inhale deeply through your nose for a count of 4.
2. Exhale slowly through your mouth for a count of 6.
3. Repeat 5 times to calm yourself.

Step Away

1. **Recognize Your Anger:** Acknowledge when you're feeling angry. It's important to be aware of your emotions as a first step.
2. **Step Away from the Situation:** Physically remove yourself from the environment or situation that's triggering your anger. Find a quiet, neutral space where you can calm down.
3. **Use Relaxation Techniques:** While taking a break, engage in relaxation techniques like deep breathing, counting to ten, or progressive muscle relaxation to calm your nerves. Focus on your breath and allow your anger to subside before returning to the situation.

Use "I" Statements

1. **Identify Your Feelings:** Take a moment to recognize and label your emotions. Understand what specifically is making you angry.
2. **Express Your Feelings with "I" Statements:** Share your emotions and concerns using "I" statements, such as "I feel frustrated when..." or "I'm upset because..." This helps take ownership of your emotions and avoids blaming others.
3. **Clearly Communicate Your Needs:** After expressing your feelings, explain what you need or what would help you feel better. For example, "I need some space right now to cool off," or "I'd appreciate it if we could discuss this calmly."

Calming Affirmations

1. **Choose Calming Affirmations:** Select affirmations that resonate with you and can help calm your anger. Examples include: "I am in control of my emotions," "I choose peace and serenity," or "I release anger and embrace calmness."
2. **Repeat and Breathe:** Take a few deep breaths to center yourself. Then, repeat your chosen affirmations slowly and deliberately. Focus on each word and the positive feelings they evoke. Continue this practice until you feel your anger subsiding and a sense of calmness taking over.

Anger Dissipation Visualization

1. **Visualize Anger Dissipation:** In your mind's eye, visualize your anger as a tangible object or energy. Imagine it gradually dissipating, like clouds dispersing in the sky or water flowing away in a stream. Focus on the sensation of relief and calmness as your anger gradually diminishes. Continue this visualization until you feel more at ease and in control of your emotions.

Physical Activity

1. **Select an Activity:** Choose a physical activity that you enjoy and can do at the moment. Do a few minutes of stretching, or even a short burst of aerobic exercise like jumping jacks.
2. **Engage in the Activity:** Start performing the chosen physical activity with intention. Focus on your movements and the physical sensations in your body as you engage in the activity.
3. **Release Tension and Breathe:** As you exercise, use this time to release built-up tension and frustration. Take deep breaths, exhaling forcefully with each breath to release pent-up energy. Allow the physical activity to help calm your nerves and bring your emotions under control.

Shake Your Body

1. **Find a Safe Space:** Locate a private and safe area where you won't be disturbed. Ensure there are no obstacles around that you might accidentally bump into.
2. **Start Shaking:** Stand with your feet shoulder-width apart, and begin shaking your body. You can start with your hands and arms and gradually let the shaking spread to your legs, hips, and the rest of your body. Imagine shaking off the tension and anger as you do this.
3. **Combine with Deep Breathing:** While shaking, take slow and deep breaths. Inhale deeply through your nose and exhale forcefully through your mouth. Continue shaking and breathing for a few minutes or until you feel a sense of release and calmness.

Use Your Strength

1. **Perform 10 Push-Ups:** Lower your body by bending your elbows while keeping your back straight. Go down until your chest is close to the ground, and then push back up to the starting position. Repeat this movement 10 times.
2. **Breathe and Reflect:** After completing the 10 push-ups, take a moment to catch your breath. Focus on your breath and allow yourself to reflect on the anger you may have been feeling. Physical activity like push-ups can help release tension and provide a sense of relief.

Calming Yoga Poses

Find a quiet, clutter-free space where you can practice without distractions. This could be your bedroom, a corner of your living room, or even a spot in your backyard.

Put on comfortable clothing that allows you to move freely. Yoga leggings or shorts and a breathable top are ideal. Ensure your clothing doesn't restrict your movements.

Create a calming atmosphere by dimming the lights, playing soft instrumental music, or lighting a scented candle if you like. This sets the tone for a relaxing practice.

Start with a gentle warm-up to prepare your body for yoga. Begin with some light stretching or joint rotations. For example, rotate your wrists, ankles, and gently twist your torso to the left and right.

Stand tall with your feet hip-width apart, arms at your sides, and palms facing forward. Close your eyes and take several deep breaths. Feel the ground beneath your feet, lengthen your spine, and relax your shoulders. This pose helps you find balance and stability.

Kneel on the floor with your big toes touching and knees apart. Sit back on your heels, extend your arms forward, and rest your forehead on the mat. Breathe deeply and let go of any tension in your body. This pose is excellent for relaxation.

Get on your hands and knees in a tabletop position. Inhale as you arch your back and lift your head (Cow Pose). Exhale as you round your back and tuck your chin (Cat Pose). Flow between these two poses for a few breaths to relieve tension in your spine.

From the tabletop position, push your hips up and back, straightening your legs. Form an inverted V shape with your body. Stretch your arms forward and relax your head between your shoulders. This pose releases tension in the back and promotes overall relaxation.

Return to Child's Pose for a moment to rest and reset. Breathe deeply and feel the gentle stretch in your lower back and shoulders.

Lie flat on your back, arms at your sides, palms facing up, and legs comfortably apart. Close your eyes and relax your entire body. Focus on your breath, letting go of any remaining tension. Stay in this pose for several minutes, enjoying a sense of deep relaxation and peace.

To conclude your practice, gently roll to one side and use your hands to push yourself up to a seated position. Take a few deep breaths before opening your eyes.

These stress-reducing yoga poses can help you relax, release tension, and improve your overall well-being. Regular practice can enhance your coping skills and help you manage stress more effectively.

Creative Writing for Anger Release

You see, creative writing isn't just about stories or poems; it's about giving your thoughts and feelings a voice. When you write, you have a safe place to express yourself without judgment. It's like having a conversation with a trusted friend who listens without interruption.

Writing lets you pour out your emotions, like venting frustrations or sharing hopes. It's like a conversation with yourself, a way to let go of what's weighing you down.

Through writing, you'll learn more about yourself and uncover your strengths, resilience, and unique perspective on the world. This self-discovery can be empowering. Writing can also be your escape. It can transport you to new worlds, real or imagined, giving you a break from stress and a chance to explore your imagination.

So, let's start this journey of self-discovery and anger relief through creative writing. You're about to discover the incredible power of your own words. Let's get started!

Gather Your Writing Materials: Collect your preferred writing materials, such as a notebook and pen, or a computer. Ensure you have a comfortable space for writing.

Reflect on Your Emotions: Take a moment to reflect on your emotions. What are you feeling right now? Acknowledge and accept these feelings without judgment.

Example: "I'm feeling a mix of frustration and sadness today. I had a challenging day at school, and it's been hard to shake off these emotions."

Choose a Writing Style: Decide on a writing style that matches your emotions. You can write in the form of journaling, poetry, short stories, or letters to yourself.
Example: Feeling particularly poetic, you decide to write a poem about your emotions.

Start Writing: Begin writing freely, allowing your emotions to flow onto the page. Write about what's bothering you, what you're grateful for, or any thoughts that come to mind.

Express Your Emotions: Express your emotions honestly and without holding back. Let the words reflect the depth of your feelings.
Example: Allow your poetry to convey the intensity of your emotions, whether through vivid imagery or raw words.

Edit and Revise (Optional): If you wish, you can edit and revise your writing later. But for this exercise, the focus is on expression, not perfection.
Example: Decide to leave the poem as is, capturing the raw emotion of the moment.

Reflect on Your Writing: After you've finished, take a moment to reflect on what you've written. How do you feel now? Has the act of writing provided any emotional release or clarity?
Example: "Writing this poem helped me process my emotions. I feel a bit lighter and more in touch with what's been bothering me."

Save Your Writing: Keep your writing in a safe place, whether it's a dedicated journal or a digital document. You might want to revisit it in the future for reflection.
Example: Place the poem in your special journal, knowing it's a record of your emotional journey.

Repeat as Needed: Creative writing for emotional release is a valuable self-care tool. Whenever you're grappling with emotions, return to this practice to express and explore them.
Example: Make a commitment to return to your creative writing whenever you need a release or a way to connect with your emotions.

Use the Thought Bubble for a Clear Mind

The Thought Bubble Exercise is a handy practice just for you. In this exercise, you'll discover a simple way to manage your thoughts and emotions effectively. Picture your thoughts as colorful bubbles floating in your mind, and you'll learn how to observe them without judgment. This exercise helps you gain clarity, reduce stress, and keep a peaceful state of mind. It's like having a secret tool to enhance your self-awareness and navigate the challenges of your teenage years more smoothly.

Find Your Space:
Begin by finding a quiet and comfortable space where you won't be disturbed. This could be your bedroom, a cozy nook, or a peaceful spot in the park.

Get Comfortable:
Sit or lie down in a position that feels relaxing for you. Make sure you're at ease and can fully focus on your thoughts.

Take Deep Breaths:
Begin with a few deep, calming breaths. Inhale slowly through your nose, allowing your chest and abdomen to rise, and then exhale through your mouth, releasing any tension.

Example: Inhale deeply for a count of four, hold for a moment, and then exhale slowly for a count of six.

Observe Your Thoughts:

Let your thoughts flow naturally. Imagine each thought appearing as a colorful bubble in your mind. Watch as these thought bubbles rise to the surface.

Example: Thoughts about a school project, an upcoming family gathering, and a fun weekend plan all appear as different bubbles in your mind.

Non-Judgmental Observation:

Observe each thought bubble without judgment. Allow them to float by, acknowledging their presence without attaching any labels or emotions to them.

Example: You notice the school project bubble and let it drift away without worrying about it.

Letting Go:

If a thought feels stressful or overwhelming, imagine it gently floating away, disappearing into the distance. Trust that you can return to it when needed.

Example: The thought of the upcoming family gathering, which feels a bit stressful, floats away, leaving your mind clear and peaceful.

Return to Your Breath:

Whenever you need to refocus or calm your mind, return your attention to your breath. Use it as an anchor to stay present.

Example: If you notice your mind wandering, simply go back to the sensation of your breath entering and leaving your body.

Express Gratitude:

Before concluding the exercise, take a moment to express gratitude for this time of self-care. Recognize the clarity and calmness you've cultivated.

Example: You feel grateful for the peace and relaxation you've found during this exercise.

Slowly Return:

When you're ready, slowly open your eyes and return to your surroundings. Take a deep breath and carry this sense of clarity and calmness with you.

Example: You open your eyes feeling refreshed and ready to continue your day with a clear mind.

Stress-Relief Through Music

Tune into Your Emotions

Begin by acknowledging your current emotional state. Take a moment to recognize and name the feelings you're experiencing. Are you stressed, anxious, happy, or sad?

Example: You recognize that you're feeling a bit anxious due to upcoming exams.

Select Your Soundtrack

Choose a piece of music that matches your emotions or the emotional state you'd like to achieve. Whether it's calming, energizing, or uplifting, your soundtrack should resonate with you.

Example: You opt for a soothing instrumental track to help calm your anxiety.

Create a Musical Oasis

Transform your listening space into a soothing oasis. Dim the lights, light a scented candle, or arrange some cozy cushions to enhance the ambiance.

Dive into the Melody

Put on your chosen music and focus your attention entirely on the sounds. Listen closely to the instruments, melodies, and rhythms.

Express Yourself Through Movement

Let the music inspire your movements. You can sway, dance, or even create your own rhythmic motions to release pent-up tension.

Explore Your Emotions
Pay attention to how the music affects your emotions. Are you feeling more relaxed, joyful, or centered? Embrace these emotional shifts.

Example: The calming instrumental music gradually eases your anxiety, and you start to feel more relaxed.

Reflect and Release
After your musical journey, take a moment to reflect on your experience. Write down any thoughts or emotions that surfaced during the exercise, and if you wish, release any lingering stress or worries onto the paper.

Example: You jot down how the music helped alleviate your anxiety and allowed you to focus on the present moment.

Use Your Senses to Reduce Stress

1.Mindful Observation

Focus on one of your senses, such as sight. Take a moment to look around and notice the colors, shapes, and textures in your environment. Observe without judgment.

Example: You notice the vibrant colors of the flowers outside your window and the intricate patterns on your desk.

2.Engage Your Sense of Touch

Shift your attention to your sense of touch. What do you feel against your skin or in your surroundings? It might be the warmth of sunlight, the softness of a blanket, or the texture of a nearby object.

Example: You run your fingers across the soft fabric of your blanket, feeling its comforting texture.

3.Explore Sounds

Tune in to the sounds around you. What do you hear? Listen to both distant and nearby sounds, without trying to identify or label them.

Example: You hear birds singing outside, the faint hum of your computer, and the gentle rustling of leaves in the wind.

4.Savor Taste

If you have a small snack or drink nearby, take a moment to savor it mindfully. Pay attention to the flavors, textures, and sensations as you eat or drink.

Example: You enjoy a piece of dark chocolate, noticing its rich taste and how it slowly melts in your mouth.

5.Inhale Aromas

If there's a pleasant scent nearby, bring it close to your nose and take a deep breath. Focus on the aroma and how it makes you feel.

Example: You pick up a lavender-scented sachet and inhale deeply, letting the calming aroma fill your senses.

6.Reflect on Your Senses

Take a moment to reflect on how engaging your senses made you feel. Did it help you relax or shift your focus away from stress? Embrace the present moment and the sensory experiences you've explored.

Example: You realize that paying attention to your senses helped you feel more grounded and less stressed. It provided a welcome break from your worries.

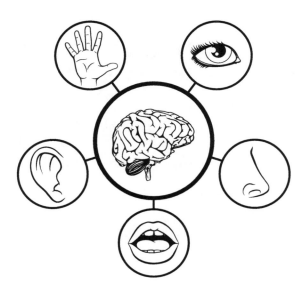

Block Your Time to Reduce Stress

Do you ever find yourself juggling a long list of tasks and feeling overwhelmed by the ticking clock? Well, you're not alone. Time management can be a game-changer, especially for teenagers with busy schedules. That's where the time-boxing method comes in.

Imagine having a clear plan for your day, with specific time slots dedicated to each activity. It's like having your own superhero sidekick, helping you tackle tasks efficiently and reduce stress. In this exercise, you'll discover how time-boxing can be your secret weapon for staying on top of things, leaving you more time to relax and enjoy life. So, let's dive in and learn how this method can make your day-to-day routine smoother and less stressful.

1.Set Clear Priorities
Begin by listing the most important tasks or activities you need to complete during the day. These could be homework assignments, study sessions, extracurricular activities, or even relaxation time.

Example: You jot down tasks like finishing a math assignment, studying for a history test, attending soccer practice, and spending time with family.

2.Determine Your Available Time
Estimate how much time you have available for your tasks. Be realistic about the time you can allocate, considering school hours, meal breaks, and any other commitments.

Example: You calculate that you have around 5 hours in the afternoon and evening after school and dinner.

3.Create Time Blocks
Divide your available time into blocks, each dedicated to a specific task or activity. Make sure to include short breaks in between to rest and recharge.

Example: You create time blocks, such as 45 minutes for math homework, 30 minutes for history study, a 15-minute break, 1 hour for soccer practice, and 30 minutes for family time.

4.Set Clear Start and End Times

Assign precise start and end times to each time block. This helps you maintain focus and prevents tasks from running longer than planned.

Example: You decide to start your math homework at 4:00 PM and finish by 4:45 PM, followed by history study from 4:50 PM to 5:20 PM.

5.Use a Planner or Digital Tool

Record your time blocks in a planner or use a digital tool, like a calendar app, to keep track of your schedule. Make sure it's easily accessible and visible.

Example: You input your time blocks into your smartphone's calendar app and set up reminders.

6.Stay Flexible

While sticking to your time blocks, remain open to necessary adjustments. If a task takes longer than expected or if you need more break time, adapt your schedule accordingly.

Example: You realize that your math assignment is more challenging than anticipated, so you extend the time block by 15 minutes.

7.Reflect and Adjust

At the end of the day, review how well you followed your time blocks. Celebrate your accomplishments and identify areas where you can improve your time management for the next day.

Example: You notice that your soccer practice ran late, causing a delay in your family time. You decide to allocate more buffer time between activities in the future to avoid feeling rushed.

Practice Compassionate Self-Talk

1 **Self-Awareness Check-In**

Begin by pausing for a moment to check in with your current emotional state. Are you feeling stressed, anxious, or overwhelmed? Acknowledge your feelings without judgment.

Example: You recognize that you're feeling stressed about an upcoming test.

2 **Identify Negative Self-Talk**

Pay attention to any negative thoughts or self-talk that might be contributing to your stress. These could be thoughts like, "I can't do this," or "I'm going to fail."

Example: You catch yourself thinking, "I'll never be able to remember all this information."

3 **Challenge Negative Thoughts**

Challenge these negative thoughts by questioning their accuracy. Ask yourself if there's evidence to support these beliefs or if they're just unhelpful assumptions.

Example: You ask, "Is it really true that I can't remember the information, or am I just feeling overwhelmed right now?"

4 **Reframe with Positive Self-Talk**

Replace the negative self-talk with more positive and realistic statements. Encourage and support yourself. Use phrases like, "I can handle this," or "I'm capable of learning."

Example: You reframe your thought to, "I might find this challenging, but I can break it down into smaller steps and learn it."

5 Breathe and Relax

Take a few deep breaths to calm your mind and body. Inhale slowly through your nose, and exhale gently through your mouth. Allow yourself to relax as you repeat your positive self-talk.

Example: You take a deep breath and say to yourself, "I can handle this. I've faced tough challenges before."

6 Visualize Success

Close your eyes and visualize yourself successfully managing the situation that's causing you stress. Imagine yourself feeling confident and capable.

Example: You visualize yourself answering test questions with ease and a sense of accomplishment.

7 Self-Compassion

Practice self-compassion by reminding yourself that it's okay to feel stressed sometimes. Treat yourself with kindness and understanding, as you would a friend going through a tough time.

Example: You say to yourself, "It's okay to feel stressed about the test. I'm doing my best, and that's what matters."

8 Repeat as Needed

Whenever negative self-talk creeps in, repeat this process to challenge and reframe your thoughts. Over time, it can become a habit that helps you manage stress more effectively.

Example: During the test, if you start to feel anxious, you remind yourself of your positive self-talk and take a deep breath to regain your composure.

Anxiety Coping Skills through Self-Reflection and Growth

Values Clarification Exercise

PRIORITY

Self-Reflection
Begin by finding a quiet space where you can focus without distractions. Take a few deep breaths to center yourself and prepare for self-reflection.

Example: You find a comfortable spot in your room, close your eyes, and take a few deep breaths to calm your mind.

Identify Past Experiences
Think about some meaningful experiences or moments in your life when you felt truly content, fulfilled, or proud. These could be personal achievements, moments with friends or family, or even times spent in nature.

Example: You recall the time you volunteered at a local animal shelter and felt a deep sense of purpose and happiness.

Explore Emotions
Reflect on the emotions you felt during those experiences. What were the core feelings associated with those moments? Were you feeling joy, compassion, excitement, or something else?

Example: You realize that during your volunteer work, you felt a strong sense of compassion and fulfillment.

Identify Core Values
Based on the emotions you've identified, think about the values that were important to you in those moments. These values could include compassion, kindness, community, or personal growth.

Example: You recognize that compassion and community were central values during your volunteer experience.

Create a Values List

Write down a list of values that resonate with you. These could be values you've identified from your past experiences or ones you believe are essential in your life.

Example: You create a list that includes values like compassion, kindness, community, personal growth, and family.

Prioritize Your Values

Review your list of values and prioritize them based on their significance to you. Consider which values are most essential and align with who you want to be.

Example: After careful consideration, you decide that compassion and personal growth are your top priorities.

Set Intentions

Take a moment to set intentions for how you can incorporate your prioritized values into your daily life. Consider actions or behaviors that align with these values.

Example: You decide to practice compassion by volunteering regularly at the animal shelter and focusing on personal growth by setting specific goals for self-improvement.

Reflect and Adapt

Periodically revisit your values and intentions to ensure they continue to resonate with you. Adapt and adjust them as needed to stay aligned with your evolving goals and aspirations.

Example: You reflect on your values regularly and find that they still hold true, but you decide to expand your community involvement by joining a local environmental group, aligning with your values of compassion and community.

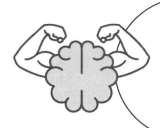

Assess and Enhance Your Strengths

Objective: This exercise encourages you to assess your strengths, identify areas for improvement, and create an action plan for enhancement through writing.

Identify Your Strengths (Write down at least three):
Begin by listing three strengths or talents you believe you possess.

Reflect on Your Strengths (Write down your reflections):
Think about situations where you've demonstrated these strengths. Write about those experiences and how they made you feel.

Assess the Impact (Write down your thoughts):
Consider how these strengths have positively influenced your life. Write down examples of times when your strengths have been valuable.

Identify Areas for Improvement (Write down areas for improvement for each strength):
For each strength, list one area or aspect you think you can improve.

Set Goals (Write down your goals - make them specific and time-bound):
For each area of improvement, set a clear and achievable goal.

Seek Resources (Write down where you can find resources):
Identify resources that can help you improve each strength. This could include books, courses, mentors, or clubs.

Plan for Practice (Write down your practice plan):
Create a plan for regularly practicing and improving your strengths.

Reflect and Adjust (Write down your reflections and any adjustments):
Periodically reflect on your progress. Write down what's working well and any adjustments you need to make.

Remember, writing down your thoughts and plans can help you stay organized and focused on enhancing your strengths effectively.

Growth Mindset Development

Understanding how role models achieve success can inspire and guide teenagers in developing a growth mindset. This exercise is designed to help teenagers analyze the journeys of their role models, learn from their experiences, and apply these lessons to their own lives.

To explore the stories of role models and identify the challenges they faced and overcame on their path to success, helping teens develop a growth mindset.

1 Choose Your Role Model
Select a role model or someone you admire. This could be a celebrity, athlete, entrepreneur, artist, or anyone who has achieved success in an area that interests you.

2 Research Your Role Model (Write down your findings):
Research your chosen role model. Look for information on their background, early life, career, and achievements. Write down key details about their journey.

3 Identify Their Challenges (Write down their challenges):
Discover and make a list of the obstacles and challenges your role model faced along the way. This could include failures, setbacks, or personal difficulties.

4 Analyze Their Response (Write down your analysis):
Consider how your role model responded to these challenges. Did they give up, or did they persevere and adapt? Write down your observations and thoughts.

5 **Highlight Their Growth Mindset** (Write down examples of their growth mindset):
Find instances where your role model exhibited a growth mindset. This could involve embracing learning opportunities, seeking feedback, or putting in extra effort. Note these examples.

6 **Reflect on Lessons Learned (Write down your reflections):**
Reflect on what you've learned from your role model's journey. How can you apply these lessons to your own life, challenges, and goals? Write down specific takeaways.

7 **Set Personal Goals (Write down your goals):**
Based on your analysis and the lessons you've learned, set one or two personal goals related to your own growth and development. Be specific and time-bound.

8 **Share and Discuss (Optional - Share with someone you trust):**
If you're comfortable, share your findings and insights with a trusted friend, family member, or mentor. Discuss how these lessons can shape your mindset and actions.

Example:
Role Model: Michelle Obama

Research Findings: Michelle Obama, the former First Lady, grew up in a working-class family in Chicago. She faced challenges related to socioeconomic background and racial discrimination.

Challenges Faced:

- Financial limitations
- Prejudice and stereotypes
- Balancing work and family
- Response to Challenges:
- Michelle Obama worked diligently in school, earning scholarships to prestigious universities. She actively addressed issues of racial inequality and later used her platform as First Lady to promote education and healthy living.

Growth Mindset Examples:

1. Continuous learning through higher education
2. Advocacy for social justice
3. Efforts to inspire healthy habits in youth

Lessons Learned: Michelle Obama's story teaches us that a growth mindset involves resilience, education, and a commitment to making a positive impact. We can apply these principles to our own lives by pursuing education, standing up for what's right, and striving to make a difference.

Personal Goal: I will actively seek educational opportunities and engage in activities that promote positive change in my community.

Receive Feedback and Grow

Seek Constructive Feedback

Choose a specific area you want to improve, such as your public speaking skills for class presentations. Ask your teacher, a classmate, or a family member if they can provide feedback on your recent presentation.

Example: Approach your teacher and request feedback on your recent class presentation about climate change.

Be Open to Feedback

When receiving feedback, actively listen and ask clarifying questions if necessary. Encourage the person giving feedback to provide specific examples or suggestions for improvement.

Example: As your teacher provides feedback, ask questions like, "Could you give me an example of where I could improve my delivery?"

Reflect on Feedback

Take some time to think about the feedback you received. Consider how it relates to your goals and what specific actions you can take to address the feedback.

Example: Reflect on your teacher's feedback, noting areas where you struggled during the presentation and where you received praise.

Set Improvement Goals

Write down at least four improvement goals based on the feedback you received. These goals should be specific, measurable, achievable, relevant, and time-bound (SMART).

Example:
- ○ Improve eye contact with the audience by maintaining it for at least 80% of the presentation.
- ○ Reduce filler words (um, like, uh) to no more than two per minute.
- ○ Enhance the organization of the presentation by using clear headings and transitions.
- ○ Practice vocal variety by emphasizing key points with changes in tone and volume.

Develop an Action Plan

Create a detailed action plan that outlines the steps you'll take to work toward your improvement goals. Break down each goal into smaller tasks.

Example: For the goal of improving eye contact, your action plan might include practicing in front of a mirror, recording yourself, and seeking peer feedback.

Implement Your Plan

Put your action plan into action. Dedicate specific time slots in your schedule to work on each aspect of your improvement goals.

Example: Schedule 30 minutes each day for practice, focusing on different aspects of your presentation skills.

Monitor Progress

Regularly assess your progress toward each improvement goal. Keep a journal or checklist to track the work you've completed.

Example: Maintain a journal where you record your daily practice sessions, noting any improvements or challenges.

Seek Ongoing Feedback

Continue seeking feedback as you make progress. Share your updated presentation or speaking attempts with someone who can provide further input.

Example: After practicing your presentation, ask a friend or family member to watch and provide feedback on your eye contact and use of filler words.

Adjust and Adapt

Be open to adjusting your action plan and goals based on the ongoing feedback and your evolving understanding of public speaking.

Example: If you notice that your vocal variety needs more work than expected, adjust your practice time accordingly.

Celebrate Growth

Recognize and celebrate the improvements you've achieved in your public speaking skills. Take pride in your hard work and the progress you've made.

Example: Celebrate by delivering a confident and engaging presentation in your next class, knowing that your efforts have paid off.

Constructive Self-Feedback

You know yourself better than anyone else does, and you have the incredible ability to guide your own growth and development. That's where self-feedback comes into play, and it can be a powerful tool for your personal growth journey.

Picture this: You've just completed a challenging school project or faced a situation that pushed you out of your comfort zone. You may have received feedback from teachers, peers, or mentors, but what about the feedback you can give yourself? Self-feedback is like having a trusted mentor within you, offering guidance, encouragement, and constructive insights.

In this journey of self-discovery and personal growth, you'll explore how to provide yourself with feedback that empowers you to improve, achieve your goals, and build resilience. Together, we'll dive into various techniques and exercises designed to help you become your own best mentor, unlocking your full potential as a confident and capable individual. So, are you ready to become the best version of yourself? Let's get started on this transformative path of self-feedback and self-discovery.

Choose a Specific Scenario
Begin by selecting a recent situation or event where you'd like to provide yourself with feedback. This could be related to school, a hobby, a project, or an interpersonal interaction.

Example: Choose a recent school presentation you gave on a topic of interest.

Set the Tone
Start your feedback letter by setting a positive and constructive tone. Begin with a friendly greeting and a statement of your intention to provide supportive feedback.

Example: "Dear [Your Name], I hope this letter finds you well. I wanted to take a moment to reflect on your recent presentation and offer some thoughts to help you grow."

Acknowledge Strengths

Recognize and acknowledge the strengths and positive aspects of your performance in the chosen scenario. Be specific and highlight what you did well.

Example: "I was impressed by your in-depth knowledge of the topic and your ability to convey your passion for it. Your introduction effectively captured the audience's attention."

Address Areas for Improvement

Identify and discuss areas where you believe there is room for improvement. Be specific and offer suggestions for how you can enhance your performance in these areas.

Example: "However, I noticed that there were moments when you could have maintained better eye contact with the audience. Consider practicing this skill to create a stronger connection."

Offer Constructive Feedback

Provide constructive feedback in a supportive manner. Avoid using negative language or criticism. Instead, frame your feedback as an opportunity for growth.

Example: "To improve your eye contact, you might try practicing in front of a mirror or recording yourself. This can help you become more comfortable maintaining eye contact with your audience."

Share Personal Insights

Share any personal insights or experiences related to the situation. Offer anecdotes or examples from your own journey that relate to the feedback you're providing.

Example: "I remember when I struggled with maintaining eye contact during presentations. What helped me was practicing with a trusted friend and gradually increasing the duration of eye contact during each practice session."

Encourage Goal Setting

Encourage yourself to set specific goals for improvement based on the feedback you've provided. Emphasize the importance of setting actionable goals.

Example: "I believe that with focused practice, you can significantly enhance your presentation skills. Consider setting a goal to maintain eye contact for at least 80% of your next presentation."

Express Support and Belief

Conclude your letter by expressing your support, belief in your abilities, and confidence that you can make positive changes based on the feedback.

Example: "Remember that I have full confidence in your abilities. You've shown dedication and passion in the past, and I believe you can excel even further with continued effort."

Sign Off with Encouragement

Sign off the letter with warm and encouraging words, reinforcing your desire to see yourself succeed and grow.

Example: "Wishing you all the best in your future endeavors. I'm excited to see how you'll shine in your next presentation!"

Keep the Letter

Keep this feedback letter in a safe place and revisit it periodically to track your progress and remind yourself of the constructive feedback you've received.

A feedback letter is a valuable self-reflection tool that can help teens develop self-awareness, set improvement goals, and maintain a positive attitude toward personal growth.

Reflect on Past Achievements

Select an Achievement
Begin by choosing a past achievement or accomplishment you're proud of. This could be an academic achievement, a personal milestone, or a project you successfully completed.

Example: Select the achievement of receiving an A grade on your challenging history research paper.

Recall the Details
Close your eyes and take a moment to vividly recall the details of this achievement. Remember the effort you put in, the challenges you faced, and the emotions you experienced.

Example: Visualize the hours you spent researching, writing, and revising your history paper. Recall the satisfaction and pride you felt when you received the A grade.

List Key Contributions
Make a list of the key contributions you made that led to this achievement. Identify the skills, qualities, and actions that played a significant role.
Example: List contributions such as thorough research, effective time management, well-structured arguments, and seeking feedback from your teacher.

Reflect on Challenges
Consider any challenges or obstacles you encountered while working toward this achievement. Reflect on how you overcame them or adapted your approach.

Example: Recall the challenge of finding credible sources for your research and how you reached out to your teacher for guidance.
sons in future endeavors.

Recognize Personal Growth

Reflect on the personal growth and skills you developed as a result of this achievement. How did it contribute to your overall development and confidence?

Example: Recognize that this achievement improved your research skills, time management, and ability to handle challenging assignments.

Set Future Goals

Based on what you've learned from this achievement, set future goals for yourself. Consider how you can apply the skills and qualities you've developed in new endeavors.

Example: Set a goal to maintain the same level of dedication and organization in your upcoming research projects.

Express Gratitude

Take a moment to express gratitude for the support and resources that contributed to your achievement. This can include thanking teachers, mentors, or family members.

Example: Write a thank-you note to your history teacher for their guidance and feedback throughout the research paper process.

Celebrate Your Achievement

Celebrate your past achievement in a meaningful way. This could involve treating yourself to something you enjoy or sharing your success with friends and family.

Example: Celebrate by having a small gathering with friends and sharing your accomplishment, or by treating yourself to a special meal.

Journal Your Reflections

Write down your reflections and insights about this achievement in a journal. Capture the lessons you've learned and the positive emotions associated with it.

Example: Journal about how this achievement boosted your confidence and how you plan to apply these lessons in future endeavors.

Explore Your Emotional Blueprint

Memory Lane
Think of a recent challenging situation or an emotional episode that bothered you. Take a moment to recall it.

Emotion Check
Identify the primary emotion you felt during that situation. Was it anger, anxiety, sadness, or something else?

Trigger Identification
Ask yourself, "What set off this emotion? Was it something someone said, a specific place, a recurring thought, or a particular circumstance?"

Physical Sensations
Reflect on any physical sensations you experienced at that moment. Did your heart race, did your palms sweat, or did you feel a knot in your stomach?

Thought Patterns
Consider the thoughts or beliefs that crossed your mind during this emotional episode. What were you telling yourself at the time?

External Influences
Think about external factors that might have contributed to your emotional response. Were there people, expectations, or environmental factors at play?

Trigger Awareness
Write down the identified trigger, your emotional response, and any associated physical sensations, thoughts, or external influences.

Strategies for Coping
Now that you've pinpointed a trigger, brainstorm strategies to deal with it constructively. What can you do next time this trigger appears?

Practice and Preparedness: Implement your chosen coping strategies when you encounter this trigger again. Practice them regularly to build your resilience.

Example: For instance, you recall feeling anxious (emotion) during a class presentation (trigger) because you believed everyone was judging your performance (thoughts). Your heart raced (physical sensation), and the presence of a critical classmate (external influence) intensified your anxiety.

Coping strategy: Next time, you decide to practice deep breathing and remind yourself of your preparation and competence (positive self-talk) to manage your anxiety during presentations.

This creative exercise helps teens explore their emotional triggers, develop awareness, and equip themselves with coping strategies to effectively navigate challenging situations in the future.

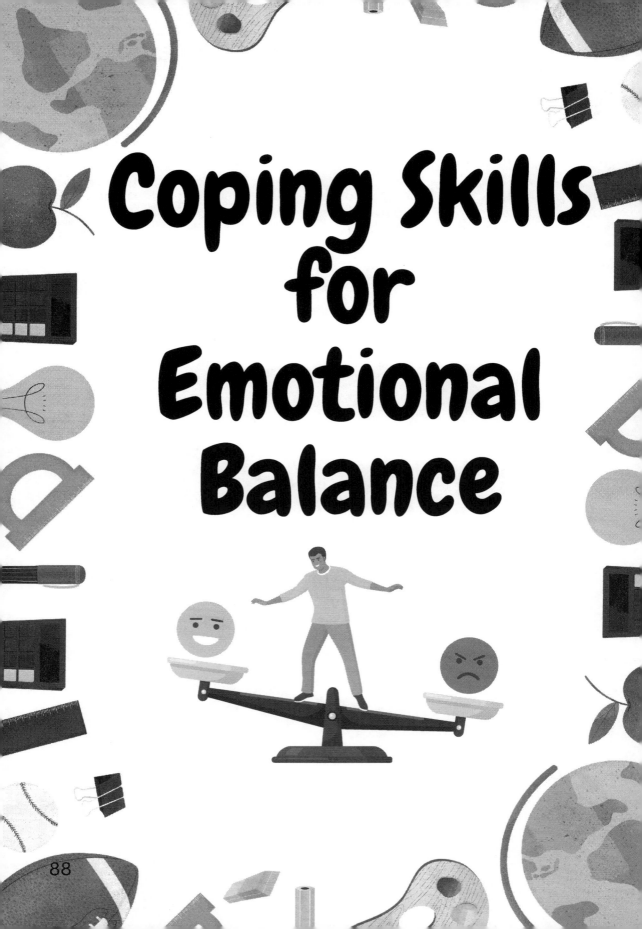

Coping Skills for Emotional Balance

Emotional Check-In Practices

Observe Your Emotions:
Look at the emotion wheel and take a moment to observe your current emotional state. Start from the center of the wheel, which often represents a neutral or calm state.

Identify Your Emotion:
Slowly move your gaze outward to the different sections of the wheel, each labeled with specific emotions. As you do this, ask yourself:
"What am I feeling right now?"
"Which emotion on the wheel best describes my current state?"

Write It Down:
Once you've identified the emotion that resonates with your current state, write it down on a piece of paper or in a journal.

Reflect on the Trigger:
Prompt yourself to reflect on what might have triggered this emotion. Write down a few sentences or keywords about the situation or thought that led to this feeling.

Explore Physical Sensations:
Consider any physical sensations associated with this emotion. Are you experiencing tension, a racing heart, or a knot in your stomach? Write down these physical cues.

Journal Your Thoughts:
Take a moment to journal about this emotion. Write down:
How intensely you're feeling it (on a scale of 1 to 10).
Whether this emotion is familiar or unusual for you.
Any thoughts or beliefs connected to this emotion.

Plan for Self-Care:
- If the emotion is challenging or uncomfortable, brainstorm self-care strategies to help you manage it. Write down a few self-care actions you can take.

Repeat as Needed:
- Whenever you feel the need to check in with your emotions, use the emotion wheel to help you identify and understand what you're feeling.
Example: As you observe the emotion wheel, you notice that the section labeled "Anxiety" best describes your current state. You write down "Anxiety" as your identified emotion.

Reflecting on the trigger, you realize that an upcoming deadline at work is causing this anxiety.

You note physical sensations like a racing heart and a sense of restlessness. In your journal, you rate the intensity of your anxiety as a 7, and you write down thoughts like, "I'm worried I won't meet the deadline."

To manage your anxiety, you plan to take short breaks, practice deep breathing, and create a to-do list to tackle the work systematically.

The Emotion Wheel exercise allows you to recognize, label, and explore your emotions, leading to better self-awareness and the ability to address your feelings constructively.

Express Your Feelings Through Creation

Gather Your Supplies
Before you begin, gather your art supplies. You might need paper, paints, colored pencils, or whatever medium you prefer.

Create a Calm Space
Find a quiet and comfortable place to work. Dim the lights, put on soothing music, and make sure you won't be disturbed.

Choose Your Emotion
Think about an emotion that's been on your mind. It could be happiness, frustration, sadness, or any feeling you want to explore.

Let Your Emotion Flow
Start creating your art, letting your chosen emotion guide your brush or pencil. Don't worry about making it perfect; focus on expressing yourself.

Think Symbolically
As you work, consider how the colors, shapes, and lines represent your emotion. What does each element convey about how you're feeling?

Connect to Triggers
If this emotion is connected to a specific trigger or situation, incorporate symbols or elements related to that trigger into your artwork.

Reflect and Write
After finishing your artwork, take a moment to reflect on the process. Consider what you've created and how it relates to your emotions and triggers.

Write down your thoughts:
What did you discover about your feelings while creating this art?
How did you represent your emotion through your artwork?
If there's a trigger, how did you symbolize it?
How might this creative process help you cope with similar emotions or triggers in the future?

Use Art as a Coping Tool

Recognize that art can be a valuable coping tool. When you experience similar emotions or triggers, return to this creative process to help you express and manage them.

Example

Let's say you choose to express your anxiety (emotion) through a drawing (medium). You draw swirling patterns and chaotic lines, symbolizing the turbulence of anxiety. As you create, you realize that your anxiety is often triggered by upcoming exams. You include images of test papers and a clock, connecting the emotion to its trigger.

Writing prompts:

"I noticed that my anxiety feels like..."
"The colors and shapes I used represent my anxiety because..."
"Incorporating the test papers and clock in my art helped me understand..."
"In the future, I can use art to..."

This exercise encourages you to use art not only as a creative outlet but also as a tool for understanding, processing, and coping with your emotions and triggers.

Daily Emotional Balance Techniques

You have incredible potential to shape your emotional well-being, and daily emotional balance techniques can be your guiding light. By making these practices a part of your daily routine, you can cultivate a sense of inner peace, resilience, and emotional strength that will empower you to navigate life's challenges with grace. In the following exercise, you'll discover how these techniques can benefit you and gain insights into how they reduce stress and improve your overall emotional health.

Setting Emotional Intentions

Choose Your Emotional Goal
Take a moment to consider the emotional state you want to cultivate today. It could be confidence, joy, calmness, or any other positive emotion.

Define Your Intention
Write down a clear and specific intention for the day. For example, "Today, I intend to feel confident and self-assured."

Identify Triggers
Reflect on potential triggers that might challenge your emotional goal. What situations or thoughts could lead to a different emotion? Write these down.

Create Affirmations
Develop affirmations that support your emotional intention. Craft statements that resonate with you and reinforce your chosen emotion.

Visualize Your Intention
Close your eyes and visualize yourself embodying your chosen emotion. Imagine how it feels, both physically and emotionally.

Develop an Action Plan
Outline specific actions you can take to align with your emotional intention. Consider how you can respond to triggers in a way that maintains your chosen emotion.

Set Time Check-Ins
Schedule brief check-ins with yourself throughout the day. During these moments, assess how well you're adhering to your emotional intention.

Adjust Your Approach
If you notice that you're straying from your intention, use these check-ins to make necessary adjustments. What can you do differently to get back on track?

Reflect at Day's End
Before going to bed, reflect on your day. Did you successfully maintain your emotional intention? What did you learn about your emotional responses?

Example: Imagine you've chosen "confidence" as your emotional goal. Your intention for the day is: "Today, I intend to feel confident and self-assured." You've identified that criticism from others can trigger self-doubt. You create an affirmation: "I am confident in my abilities, and I value my self-worth." Throughout the day, you visualize yourself confidently handling challenges. When criticism arises, you remind yourself of your affirmation.

During your check-ins, you assess your confidence level and make adjustments, such as practicing positive self-talk. In the evening, you reflect on your day, realizing that you were able to maintain your confidence and respond positively to triggers. This exercise helps you intentionally shape your emotional experiences.

Emotional Well-Being Assessment

Why should you care about this assessment? Well, think of it like this: it's a road map to your own emotional landscape. It can help you identify patterns, figure out what triggers your feelings, and even uncover your strengths.

- *How are you feeling right now, in this moment? Describe your emotions.*

- *On a scale of 1 to 10, how intense are these emotions? (1 being very mild, 10 being extremely intense)*

- *Can you pinpoint any specific events or situations that triggered these emotions?*

- *What physical sensations are you experiencing with these emotions? (e.g., tension, racing heart, stomach butterflies)*

- *Are there any recurring emotions that you've been experiencing frequently lately?*

- *Write down at least one thing you're grateful for or a recent positive experience that made you happy.*

- *Are there any emotions that you're struggling to cope with or understand?*

- *How would you describe your overall well-being today? Is it good, okay, or challenging?*

- *Think about your daily routines. Are there any activities or habits that have a noticeable impact on your emotions?*

- *What self-care actions can you plan to support your emotional well-being in the coming days?*

Create an Emotion Toolkit

These are like your secret toolkit for those tough emotional moments. They're not a way to ignore or avoid your feelings—rather, they're a way to give yourself a breather, a pause button for your emotions when they start to feel like too much to handle.

In this guide, we'll introduce you to a variety of distraction activities that you can use when you need them most. Each activity is designed to gently shift your focus away from those intense emotions, giving you a chance to catch your breath and regain your composure.

Remember, it's okay to seek help from friends, family, or professionals when you're going through a tough time. These activities are here to support you, but they're just one part of a broader toolkit for managing your emotions and well-being. So, let's dive in and explore these helpful tools together. You've got this!

Emergency Distraction Activities

Recognize the Need:
Recognize that you are experiencing strong emotions that are difficult to manage at the moment. This could be intense stress, anxiety, sadness, or anger.

Choose a Distraction Activity:
Select one of the following distraction activities or any other activity that you find enjoyable and engaging.
Coloring: Get an adult coloring book and some colored pencils or markers. Focus on filling in the intricate designs with colors.
Puzzle Solving: Work on a jigsaw puzzle or a crossword puzzle. The act of problem-solving can shift your focus.

Music Break: Put on your favorite music and have a mini dance party or simply sit and listen, paying close attention to the lyrics and melodies.

Mindful Breathing: Practice a brief mindfulness exercise by focusing solely on your breath for a few minutes. Inhale and exhale slowly, observing each breath without judgment.

Nature Observation: If possible, step outside and observe nature. Pay attention to the colors, sounds, and textures around you.

Engage Fully: Engage in the chosen activity with full attention. Try to immerse yourself in the task and let go of the troubling thoughts or emotions.

Stay Present: If your mind starts to wander back to the distressing emotions, gently guide your focus back to the activity. Remind yourself that this is a temporary distraction, and it's okay to take a break from your emotions.

Monitor Your Emotions: After engaging in the activity for a while, check in with your emotions. Are they less intense than before? Have you achieved a sense of calm or relief?

Repeat if Necessary: If you still feel overwhelmed after the first round of the distraction activity, don't hesitate to repeat the process or try a different distraction method until you feel more in control of your emotions.

Remember that these distraction activities are not a long-term solution but a helpful tool to manage intense emotions temporarily. If you find that you're struggling with your emotions frequently, it's essential to seek support from a trusted friend, family member, or mental health professional.

Positive Emotion Amplification

- Begin by finding a quiet, comfortable space where you can reflect and write without distractions.

- Take a few moments to center yourself. Close your eyes, take a few deep breaths, and let go of any tension or stress.

- Now, think about a recent positive experience or memory. It could be a moment of joy, accomplishment, love, or any other positive emotion.

- Describe this experience in detail. What happened? Who was there? How did you feel physically and emotionally?

- Next, identify the specific emotions you felt during this experience. Were you happy, grateful, excited, or content? Write down these emotions.

- Consider how this positive experience affected your thoughts and behaviors. Did it make you feel more confident, motivated, or optimistic? Note down these effects.

- Now, reflect on how you can recreate or invite more of these positive emotions into your life. What activities, people, or places tend to generate similar positive feelings for you? Write down some ideas.

- Think about how you can use this positive emotion to counterbalance challenging or negative emotions when they arise. What strategies can you employ to shift your focus towards positivity during difficult times?

- Finally, imagine how your life might improve if you consciously amplified positive emotions on a regular basis. What goals could you achieve, and how might your overall well-being be enhanced?

Example:

Think about a recent family gathering where you felt an overwhelming sense of joy and connection. During this event, you felt happy, grateful, and loved. These positive emotions made you more open and communicative with your family members, deepening your relationships. To recreate this feeling, you could schedule regular family get-togethers or engage in activities that foster connection, like game nights or shared hobbies. By consciously amplifying positive emotions, you might find that you're better equipped to cope with stress and challenges in your daily life, leading to a more fulfilling and joyful existence.

Regulate Your Emotions Through Music

Create a Playlist
Start by selecting a variety of songs that resonate with different emotions. You can use a music streaming platform or your own music library.

Identify Your Current Emotion
Take a moment to check in with yourself. What emotion are you currently feeling? It could be happiness, sadness, anger, excitement, or any other emotion.

Choose a Song
Based on your current emotion, pick a song from your playlist that matches or complements that feeling.

Listen Mindfully
Find a comfortable and quiet space to listen to the chosen song. Put on your headphones if possible to minimize distractions.

Pay Attention to Lyrics and Melodies
As you listen to the song, pay close attention to the lyrics and melodies. Notice how they make you feel and how they relate to your current emotion.

Reflect and Write
Write down your thoughts and feelings as you listen to the song. How does it affect your mood? Are there specific lyrics or musical elements that resonate with you?

Explore the Emotion
Dive deeper into the emotion you're experiencing. What triggered it? Is there something you can learn from this emotion?

Switch to a Different Song
Now, switch to a different song from your playlist that represents a contrasting emotion. For example, if you started with a sad song, switch to a happy or uplifting one.

Observe the Shift
Pay attention to how your mood shifts as you listen to the new song. Does it influence your emotional state?

Reflect and Write Again
Write down your thoughts and feelings after listening to the second song. How did it impact your emotions, and what did you learn from this exercise?

Repeat as Needed
You can continue to explore different emotions by selecting songs from your playlist and repeating this exercise as many times as you'd like.

Example: Let's say you started with a sad song that had lyrics about loss. As you listened, you found yourself reflecting on a recent personal loss, and you wrote down your feelings of sadness and longing. Then, you switched to an upbeat song with lyrics about resilience. This song gradually lifted your mood, and you wrote about feeling more hopeful and empowered. Through this exercise, you used music to navigate and regulate your emotions, gaining valuable insights into your emotional landscape.

Emotional Storytelling

Set the Scene
Find a quiet, comfortable space where you can focus without distractions. Grab a notebook, your computer, or even your smartphone for writing.

Choose an Emotion
Select an emotion you want to explore and express in your story. It could be joy, sadness, anger, or anything else you're feeling.

Craft Your Characters
Create characters for your story. They can be fictional or inspired by real people. Give them names, backgrounds, and personalities.

Build a Plot
Develop a storyline that revolves around the chosen emotion. Think about what events or situations might lead your characters to feel this way.

Dive into Descriptions
Use descriptive language to vividly portray the emotions your characters are experiencing. Show, don't just tell, what they're going through.

Embrace the Journey
Let your characters go on a journey through your story. This could involve challenges, growth, and resolution related to the chosen emotion.

Reflect on Self-Compassion
As you write, consider how self-compassion plays a role in your characters' experiences. How do they treat themselves during moments of emotional intensity?

Edit and Revise
After completing your story, review and revise it for clarity, flow, and emotional impact.

Share or Keep Private
Decide whether you want to share your emotional story with someone you trust or keep it as a private reflection.

Reflect and Learn
Take some time to reflect on what you've written and what it reveals about your own emotions and self-compassion.

Example:
Imagine you choose the emotion "sadness." You create a character named Lily who has recently experienced the loss of a beloved pet. You write about Lily's journey through grief, her memories of her pet, and her eventual acceptance of her sadness as a natural part of life. Along the way, you emphasize how Lily learns to treat herself with kindness, allowing herself to grieve without judgment. This story becomes a powerful tool for exploring and understanding your own experiences with sadness and self-compassion.

A FREE GIFT TO OUR READERS!

31 Secret Productivity Hacks & Anxiety Journal for Teens & Audiobook Full Version

Get your free gift here: